BREAKING THE STONE WALL

Get Rid Of The Beliefs That Ruin Your Life And Your Business

BY

ANDREW RICH

TABLE OF CONTENTS

FOREWORD

We all come across a "Stone Wall"—a seemingly insurmountable obstacle—along the way in life and business. The bricks of our beliefs, which are frequently imperceptible to the human eye but are incredibly potent in their ability to mold our futures, are used to build this unseen wall. We must face these deeply established beliefs head-on if we want to break free and grow since they have the power to either advance us or stand in the way of our achievement.

You will set out on a transformative journey in the pages that follow, guided by the perceptive and sympathetic author of "Breaking the Stone Wall: Get Rid Of The Beliefs That Ruin Your Life And Your Business." You will acquire the knowledge and skills necessary to eliminate the limiting ideas that have prevented you from moving forward in important areas of your life and career as a result of this in-depth guide.

For individuals who have ever questioned their capacity to accomplish their goals or who have encountered setbacks and pondered "Why me?" this book serves as a beacon of light. This book is your compass and your guide if you're aiming for athletic perfection, looking for ways to prevent injuries, curious to delve into the depths of psychological empowerment, or longing for better motivation in your business endeavors and self-improvement activities.

Each chapter serves as a portal into a world of self-discovery where you will face those pestering ideas that have been impeding your growth for far too long. The author deconstructs the many layers of our thought processes with clarity and accuracy, offering useful exercises and ways to challenge, restructure, and finally replace these self-limiting ideas with powerful ones.

In the world of fitness and exercise, you will discover how to let go of ideas that impede your physical well-being, opening the door to a healthier and more active lifestyle. You will acquire knowledge and techniques to safeguard your body as you work to achieve the highest level of performance from the part on avoiding harm.

The investigation of psychology and education will highlight the significant impact of your mindset on your personal development and teach you how to foster resilience and welcome lifelong learning. You will learn the principles of continual improvement and how to capitalize on your particular abilities in the field of training.

This book will open the doors to lasting inspiration and achievement for those navigating the frequently turbulent waters of business and entrepreneurship, enabling you to overcome difficulty and realize your professional aspirations.

Finally, you will get advice on how to break free from the chains of self-doubt and emerge as your most empowered, true self in the pursuit of self-improvement.

Prepare to face and overcome the ideas that have kept you imprisoned for too long as you go through the pages of "Breaking the Stone Wall." This book is an invitation to free yourself from self-imposed restrictions and move into a future full with opportunity.

Accept the knowledge contained within, put it to use, and get ready to see a change that goes well beyond your greatest dreams.

Your quest to a life free of self-sabotage starts right now. Welcome to the era of empowerment and self-belief. It's time to scale the Stone Wall and take control of the life and career you deserve.

With unwavering belief in your potential,

Jacob B. Walter
Editor-in-Chief

"Breaking The Stone Wall"

CHAPTER ONE

Shredding The Bad Ideas About Exercise & Sports

STEP 1: IDENTIFYING YOUR LIMITING BELIEFS

A critical first step in conquering them and reaching your fitness objectives involves acknowledging your limiting ideas about exercise and fitness.

Pay Attention to Negative Self-Talk:

Pay attention to the voice in your head that tells you not to exercise or that your fitness objectives are unachievable. You should note the precise claims it makes, such as "I'm too lazy to exercise" or "I'll never be as fit as I want to be."

Beware using expressions that convey inability or impossibility, such as "I can't," "I should," "I have to," or "I'll never." These may reveal hidden limiting beliefs.

Analyze Past Experiences:

Consider any failed attempts at exercise or fitness regimens in the past. Identify the notions or mindsets that led to such failures. For instance, if you quit working out because you thought it was too difficult, that perception may be keeping you back.

Conversely, consider any fitness victories you've experienced and the convictions that enabled you to attain those victories. By doing this, you may discover some empowering beliefs.

Identify Emotional Reactions:

When it comes to fitness and exercise, pay heed to your feelings. If you experience feelings of dread, guilt, shame, or worry, your limiting beliefs may be to blame.

Make an effort to relate these feelings to particular ideas or principles. For instance, if you feel bad about skipping an exercise, it may be because you think doing so will make you a failure.

STEP 2: CHALLENGING YOUR NEGATIVE BELIEFS

A key step in converting unhelpful or restricting attitudes into more empowering and positive ones is challenging your views about exercise and fitness.

Re-frame Negative Thoughts:

Create a contrasting, uplifting idea or belief for every unfavorable one. If you think, for instance, that you'd be too lazy to exercise, change it to "I can build an exercise routine that I enjoy and look forward to."

Repeat these affirmations—positive statements—regularly to help your mind internalize the new idea. You can repeat them to yourself every day, write them down, or post them wherever you'll see them.

Challenge Assumptions:

Analyze your beliefs critically in your mind. Ask yourself, "What evidence supports this belief, and is it really accurate?" for instance, if you think you'll never be fit. We frequently accept beliefs without examining their veracity.

Think about if your belief is supported by facts or suppositions. Are you making the assumption that you can't get fit due of your age, genetics, or other characteristics, or is there actual proof to back up this assertion?

Seek Support:

Discuss your views and objectives with a fitness coach or trainer if you have access to one. They can offer you professional advice and assist you in challenging and reshaping your views.

Spend time with people who support your optimistic outlook and fitness ambitions. Participating in a helpful group can motivate you and give you a new outlook on your beliefs.

Learn from Others:

Read or hear the success stories of people who have improved their health and fitness. Learn about the difficulties they encountered and the mental adjustments they made.

Find inspiration from fitness role models. Learn from their experiences and the ideas and tactics that made them successful.

Experiment and Adapt:

Be willing to experiment with various workout regimens, fitness pursuits, or techniques to determine which ones suit you the best. The notion that you are incapable of or uninterested in exercise can be challenged by experimentation.

Don't take any difficulties you have as evidence that your preconceived notions are true. Instead, see them as chances to modify and enhance your strategy.

It takes time to challenge your attitudes toward health and exercise. It calls for persistent work, introspection, and a dedication to changing one's perspective to one that is more optimistic and empowering. You can gradually replace limiting ideas with beliefs that promote your fitness quest and overall well being as you gather proof of your talents and accomplishments.

STEP 3: SETTING REALISTIC GOALS

For your long-term success and motivation in the area of exercise and fitness, setting reasonable goals is essential.

Unattainable objectives can cause frustration and demotivation.

Self-Assessment:

Start by evaluating how fit you are right now. Think about things like your body composition, flexibility, strength, and cardiovascular endurance.

Consider any current medical issues or physical restrictions that may have an impact on your fitness regimen. In case a medical expert's advice is required.

Define Clear Objectives:

Your fitness objectives should be as clear as you can. Instead of setting a general objective like "getting in shape," try to be more specific by setting goals like "losing 10 pounds in three months" or "running a 5K in under 30 minutes."

Make sure your objectives can be measured so you can monitor your progress. If you want to improve your strength, for instance, be specific about how much weight you want to use during each exercise.

Decide on a reasonable timetable for reaching your objectives. This promotes urgency and discourages procrastination. For instance, you might want to lose the weight in six months.

Consider Your Lifestyle:

Analyze how much time you can actually set aside each week for exercising. Regarding your schedule, employment obligations, and other duties, be truthful.

Include different workouts and pastimes that suit your interests and tastes. You'll be more likely to stick with your exercise regimen if you do this.

Set Realistic Expectations:

Be careful when making goals that call for drastic or quick changes in your way of life. Progressive change is frequently more enduring and beneficial.

Recognize that development may not always be straight-lined. Any fitness journey will inevitably experience plateaus and failures, so be ready to adjust and press on.

Keep Records:

Keep a workout and nutrition log to record your exercise regimens, eating decisions, and any alterations in your body composition or level of fitness. You may track your development using this data and make wise modifications.

A effective and long-lasting fitness journey begins with setting realistic fitness objectives. You may develop a fitness plan that is both realistic and inspiring by taking into account your present level of fitness, lifestyle, and preferences, as well as your goals. Setting attainable objectives will help you stay motivated over the long term because maintaining your fitness level is a lifelong endeavor.

CHAPTER TWO

Healing Your Mindset About Injury Prevention

STEP 1: EDUCATE YOURSELF

In order to prevent injuries in sports, exercise, and fitness, education is essential. It entails supplying people with the information and awareness they require to lower the risk of injuries sustained during physical activity.

Understanding Anatomy and Physiology

Understanding how the body functions during movement and exercise is the first step in education. Understanding principles like correct alignment, joint mechanics, and muscle function falls under this category. Understanding how the body moves and works enables people to engage in physical activity and sports with a lower chance of injury.

Proper Technique and Form:

People must be taught the proper forms and techniques for a variety of workouts and sports motions as part of education. By doing so, athletes can perform motions with less force on their muscles and joints, lowering their risk of strains, sprains, and other problems.

In many instances, individuals must get supervised instruction from certified coaches or trainers to guarantee they learn and practice good form efficiently.

Warm-Up and Cool-Down:

Warming up before exercise or sporting events is emphasized in education. The body is better prepared for physical activity with a good warm-up that increases blood flow, raises body temperature, and loosens muscles and joints.

People are instructed on the value of stretching to preserve flexibility and avoid muscle stiffness and discomfort as well as cooling down after exercise to progressively drop heart rate.

Equipment and Gear:

Education enables people to comprehend the significance of using the appropriate gear and equipment for their chosen activity. Wearing improper or ill-fitting equipment can make injuries more likely.

Wearing protective equipment like helmets or padding is crucial when participating in several activities, such as cycling or football. Individuals are made aware of these safety precautions through education.

Training Progression:

People are taught the value of increasing exercise volume and intensity gradually. Injury from overuse can result from abruptly switching from low to high intensity. Education enables people to comprehend the value of perseverance and a steady rise in workload.

In order to minimize over training and overuse injuries, education places a strong emphasis on rest and recovery. It's important to know when to push yourself and when to rest.

Nutrition and Hydration:

The function of nutrition in preventing injuries is one of the topics covered in education. The health of your muscles, bones, and energy levels are all supported by proper nutrition.

To avoid heat-related illnesses and maintain healthy body processes, it's crucial to stay hydrated. Education makes sure people are conscious of their hydration requirements when exercising.

Recognizing Warning Signs:

Education educates people to spot early injury indicators including lingering discomfort, edema, or a reduction in range of motion. Understanding these symptoms enables early intervention and the averting of more serious damage.

Recovery and Rehabilitation:

Understanding the significance of effective injury treatment and rehabilitation is part of education. This involves being aware of when to seek medical help, adhering to recommended treatment regimens, and safely resuming exercise.

Psychological Factors:

Additionally, mental aspects of injury prevention, such as stress reduction and relaxation strategies, may be covered in education. Encouraging focused, safe activity, and reducing tension and anxiety can indirectly aid in injury prevention.

In conclusion, education is a fundamental component in preventing injuries in sports, exercise, and fitness. It gives people the information and abilities they need to make wise decisions, exercise safely, and lower their chance of getting hurt. A well-informed approach to physical activity considerably adds to injury prevention and overall well-being, whether through professional coaching, fitness programs, or self-education.

STEP 2: HAVING THE RIGHT TECHNIQUE

When it comes to sports, exercise, and fitness, proper technique is essential for preventing injuries. Using the proper form and technique makes sure that your body moves effectively and safely, which lowers the risk of injury. The significance of using good technique and how to do so are explained in depth here:

Understanding the Importance of Proper Technique:

By appropriately distributing the stress across muscles and joints with proper form, overuse problems and the danger of strains and sprains are avoided.

Exercises or sports activities can be carried out more effectively with the use of proper technique, which can improve performance and lower the risk of fatigue-related injuries.

A fall and the resulting injuries are less likely when a person uses good form to preserve balance and stability.

Learn from a Qualified Instructor or Coach:

Consider working with an experienced coach or instructor if you're new to a sport or activity. They may give you on-the-spot feedback while also instructing you on the fundamentals of good technique. Attend training seminars, workshops, or classes where you can study and practice good form under the guidance of a professional.

Start with the Basics:

With each exercise or action, start with the fundamentals. This covers alignment, posture, and body positioning.

Try not to jump right into large weights or complicated moves before you have mastered the fundamentals.

Focus on Body Positioning:

When performing workouts or sports motions, keep your body in the most effective alignment. Maintaining a neutral or balanced position for the spine, head, and limbs is frequently required for this.

To protect your lower back and support your spine, contract your core muscles.

Mindful Movement:

Instead of focusing on quantity or speed, pay attention to the quality of your movements. Maintaining appropriate technique is made easier by mindfulness.

Exercises should not be performed using momentum. Instead, make deliberate motions to properly activate the desired muscles.

Consult a Health care Professional:

Consult a medical expert or physical therapist if you feel you may have been injured or are experiencing chronic pain for a full assessment and advice or how to recover.

The cornerstone of injury prevention in sports, exercise, and fitness is proper technique. The advantages of physical activity can be maximized while the risk of injuries that could hinder your fitness goals can be reduced by putting emphasis on proper form.

STEP 3: GRADUAL PROGRESSION

In the context of sports, exercise, and fitness, gradual development is a key concept in injury prevention. It entails gradually raising the duration, difficulty, or intensity of your workouts in a safe manner. This method, which allows your body to adapt and grow more resilient without overtaxing it, is crucial for lowering the risk of accidents.

Start Slowly:

Start with a manageable degree of intensity when starting a new exercise or fitness routine or when getting back into it after a hiatus. This could be working out with lesser weights, performing fewer repetitions, or moving more slowly.

Progression Over Time:

Increase the difficulty of your workouts gradually as your body adjusts to the stress. This could entail lifting heavier weights, performing more reps or sets, or doing aerobic exercises for longer periods of time.

Proper Form:

Keep proper form and technique in mind as you exercise. Incorrect form can lead to overuse strains and injuries. If you're unsure of the right form, seek advice from an experienced trainer.

Individualized Approach:

Recognize that each person's rate of development is unique. The progression used by your friend or workout partner might not be appropriate for you. Pay attention to your body's signals and modify as necessary.

STEP 4: LISTENING TO YOUR BODY

The key to injury prevention in sports, exercise, and fitness is listening to your body, which entails being attuned to the signals and sensations your body sends during physical activity. By paying attention and responding appropriately, you can reduce the risk of injuries.

Pain vs. Discomfort:

Recognize the difference between pain (sharp, uncomfortable sensations) and discomfort (such as muscle tiredness). While discomfort is common during workouts, pain may be a sign of a problem. If you feel pain, stop or change what you're doing.

Respect Pain:

Don't push through pain. Ignoring pain can lead to more serious injuries. Instead, identify the source of pain and adjust your technique or intensity accordingly.

Stretch Safely:

Stretching can improve flexibility and prevent injuries, but avoid overstretching or bouncing in stretches, which can cause harm.

Stay Hydrated and Fuel Properly:

Dehydration and inadequate nutrition can make you more susceptible to injuries. Ensure you're properly hydrated and fueled before, during, and after exercise.

Listen to Chronic Issues:

If you have chronic conditions or recurring injuries, consult a healthcare professional or physical therapist for guidance. They can help you manage these issues safely.

Rest and Recovery:

Give your body time to recover between workouts. Rest and sleep are essential for healing and preventing overuse injuries.

In summary, gradual progression and listening to your body are integral components of injury prevention in sports, exercise, and fitness. By progressively increasing the demands of your workouts while respecting your body's signals and responding appropriately, you can minimize the risk of injuries and enjoy a safe and effective fitness journey.

STEP 5: START CROSS-TRAINING

Cross-training is a comprehensive and versatile approach to injury prevention in sports, exercise, and fitness. It involves diversifying your training regimen by incorporating a variety of exercises, activities, and movements into your routine.

Diversification of Exercises:

Cross-training encourages you to participate in different forms of physical activity. This could include aerobic exercises like running, cycling, or swimming, strength training, flexibility exercises like yoga or Pilates, and activities such as dance, martial arts, or team sports.

One of the primary benefits of cross-training is that it reduces the risk of overuse injuries. Overuse injuries occur when you repeatedly stress the same muscles and joints without adequate recovery time, leading to strain and damage.

Balanced Muscle Development:

Cross-training targets a broader range of muscle groups compared to focusing solely on one type of exercise. This balanced approach helps prevent muscle imbalances, which can lead to injuries.

Engaging in different activities challenges your body to stabilize itself in various ways, improving balance and coordination. This can reduce the risk of falls and related injuries.

Improved Flexibility and Mobility:

Different exercises and activities require your body to move in various directions and patterns. This helps improve overall flexibility and joint mobility, reducing the risk of strains and sprains.

Enhanced flexibility can help your body absorb impact and stress more effectively, making it less susceptible to injuries during high-impact activities.

Enhanced Cardiovascular Fitness:

Cross-training allows you to include a variety of cardiovascular exercises in your routine, which can boost your overall cardiovascular fitness without excessive strain on specific joints or muscle groups.
A well-rounded cardiovascular fitness program can contribute to better heart health and reduce the risk of cardiovascular-related injuries.

Mental and Psychological Benefits:

Engaging in different activities keeps your workouts interesting and reduces the risk of exercise burnout or boredom, making it more likely that you'll stick to your fitness routine.

Cross-training challenges your mind by learning new skills and adapting to different workouts. This mental flexibility can enhance your overall psychological resilience and motivation.

Injury Rehabilitation and Recovery:

Cross-training can be instrumental in injury rehabilitation. When you're recovering from a specific injury, you can modify your routine to incorporate exercises that don't aggravate the injured area while maintaining your overall fitness.

Engaging in low-impact cross-training activities, like swimming or gentle yoga, can promote blood flow, reduce muscle soreness, and aid in the recovery process after intense workouts.

Customized for Individual Needs:

Cross-training allows you to tailor your fitness routine to your specific needs and goals. You can select activities that complement your primary sport or exercise while addressing any weaknesses or vulnerabilities in your body.

Preventing Burnout:

By periodically switching up your activities, cross-training prevents the monotony of doing the same exercises repeatedly. This can reduce the risk of mental and physical burnout.

In summary, cross-training is a multifaceted strategy for injury prevention in sports, exercise, and fitness. By diversifying your workouts, you reduce the risk of overuse injuries, promote balanced muscle development, improve flexibility and mobility, enhance cardiovascular fitness, and enjoy various mental and psychological benefits. It also offers opportunities for injury rehabilitation and recovery while allowing you to tailor your fitness regimen to your unique needs and goals. Cross-training is a valuable tool for maintaining a healthy and injury-resistant body.

CHAPTER THREE

Re-Framing Your Mind

STEP 1: KNOW THE LIMITING BELIEF

Identifying limiting beliefs in the context of psychology and education involves recognizing the negative or self-defeating thoughts and assumptions that can hinder your personal and academic growth. These beliefs can limit your potential, self-esteem, and success in various educational pursuits. Here's a detailed explanation of how to identify limiting beliefs in psychology and education:

Academic History:

Reflect on your academic history, including any past challenges, failures, or successes. Consider how these experiences may have shaped your beliefs about your abilities.

Note any areas where your beliefs have changed or evolved over time. What influenced these changes?

Emotional Responses:

Monitor your emotional responses to academic situations. Feelings of fear, frustration, or self-doubt can be indicators of limiting beliefs.

Identify specific situations, subjects, or tasks that trigger negative emotions. These can help pinpoint the beliefs that need addressing.

Ask "Why" and Challenge Assumptions:

Challenge your negative beliefs by asking questions like, "Why do I believe this?" or "What evidence supports this belief?"

Examine whether your beliefs are based on actual evidence or unfounded assumptions. Often, we hold onto beliefs without critically evaluating their validity.

Listen to Self-Talk:

Pay close attention to your inner dialogue during academic tasks. Are you using negative self-talk or self-criticism? Identify the specific statements you make to yourself.

Join Support Groups:

Connect with others who share similar academic experiences and challenges. Peer support groups can provide encouragement, empathy, and strategies for addressing limiting beliefs.

If you struggle to identify or address your limiting beliefs on your own, consider seeking the assistance of a therapist or counselor. They can provide guidance and techniques to delve into the root causes of these beliefs.

Identifying limiting beliefs in psychology and education is a process of self-awareness and critical self-examination. By recognizing these beliefs and understanding their origins, you can take steps to challenge and reframe them, ultimately empowering yourself to achieve greater success and personal growth in your educational pursuits.

STEP 2: DEVELOP A GROWTH MINDSET

A growth mindset is a psychological concept developed by psychologist Carol Dweck. It refers to the belief that one's abilities and intelligence are not fixed traits but can be developed and improved over time with effort, learning, and perseverance. In the context of psychology and education, a growth mindset has profound implications for how individuals approach challenges, setbacks, and learning.

Belief in Development:

In contrast to a fixed mindset, where individuals believe their abilities are static, those with a growth mindset believe in the potential for development. They understand that intelligence, talents, and skills can be cultivated through dedication and hard work.

Embracing Challenges:

Individuals with a growth mindset tend to view challenges as opportunities for growth and learning rather than as threats to their self-esteem. They understand that facing difficulties can lead to improvement.

Effort as the Path to Mastery:

People with a growth mindset appreciate the role of effort in achieving mastery. They see that putting in the time and energy to learn and practice is essential for progress.

Resilience in the Face of Setbacks:

A growth mindset fosters resilience in the face of setbacks. Instead of giving up when confronted with failures or mistakes, individuals with this mindset see setbacks as temporary and a chance to learn.

They actively seek lessons in failures and use them to adapt and improve. This approach can lead to increased confidence and motivation.

Openness to Learning:

A growth mindset promotes a commitment to lifelong learning. It encourages individuals to continue acquiring knowledge and skills throughout their lives, realizing that growth and improvement are ongoing processes.

Mastery Over Time:

In education, students with a growth mindset are more likely to embrace incremental progress. They understand that improvement may not always be rapid but that consistent effort leads to mastery over time.

A growth mindset allows students to adapt to new challenges and subjects more readily. They believe in their capacity to learn and tackle unfamiliar material.

Reduction of Anxiety and Fear:

Students with a growth mindset often experience reduced performance anxiety because they see assessments as opportunities to learn rather than as judgments of their inherent ability.

Creating a Culture of Growth:

In educational settings, cultivating a growth mindset can create a culture of growth and learning. Teachers and instructors can encourage this mindset by praising effort and persistence rather than innate ability.

Providing constructive and supportive feedback that focuses on effort and improvement can motivate students to adopt and maintain a growth mindset.

In summary, a growth mindset is a powerful psychological concept that promotes the belief in the potential for development and improvement. In the realm of education and psychology, it encourages individuals to embrace challenges, persist through setbacks, and value effort as the path to mastery. This mindset not only enhances learning and performance but also fosters resilience, reduces anxiety, and creates a culture of growth and lifelong learning.

STEP 3: KEEP LEARNING

Continuous learning is a vital concept in the fields of psychology and education. It refers to the ongoing process of acquiring new knowledge, skills, and insights throughout one's life, even after formal education has ended.

Lifelong Learning Philosophy:

Continuous learning is based on the belief that learning should be a lifelong pursuit. It recognizes that knowledge and understanding in the fields of psychology and education are constantly evolving.

As society, technology, and research progress, new insights and best practices emerge. Continuous learning ensures that professionals in psychology and education remain adaptable and up-to-date.

Adaptation to Changing Needs:

The student and client populations in psychology and education are diverse, with unique needs and challenges. Continuous learning helps professionals adapt their approaches to meet these evolving needs.

Cultural sensitivity and competence are increasingly important in these fields. Continuous learning includes training in cultural awareness and the ability to work effectively with individuals from various backgrounds.

Personal Growth and Fulfillment:

Continuous learning provides intellectual stimulation and personal fulfillment. It fosters curiosity, critical thinking, and a passion for discovery.

Professionals who engage in continuous learning are often better equipped to solve complex problems, make informed decisions, and find innovative solutions to challenges in their work.

Continuous learning in psychology and education is a commitment to ongoing personal and professional development. It ensures that professionals remain knowledgeable, skilled, and adaptable, leading to improved outcomes for their clients and students. It also fosters personal growth, a broader perspective, and a deeper understanding of the complexities of human behavior and learning. Continuous learning is not just a choice; it's a necessity for those dedicated to making a positive impact in these fields.

STEP 4: BE AROUND POSITIVE ENERGY

Surrounding yourself with positivity in the context of psychology and education can have a significant impact on your mental well-being, personal growth, and educational success.

Choose Supportive Relationships:

Seek out friends, family members, mentors, or peers who are positive influences in your life. These individuals should be supportive, encouraging, and nurturing of your goals and personal development.

Minimize contact with people who consistently bring negativity or doubt into your life. Negative influences can hinder your progress and impact your self-esteem.

Create a Supportive Environment:

Arrange your physical environment to promote positivity. A clean, organized, and aesthetically pleasing space can enhance your mood and overall well-being.

Decluttering your space can also declutter your mind, making it easier to focus on your educational pursuits and personal growth.

Seek Positive Educational Experiences:

When selecting courses or educational programs, consider those that align with your interests and passions. Engaging with subjects you enjoy can make learning more enjoyable and fulfilling.

Actively engage in your educational experiences. Join discussions, collaborate with classmates, and take part in extracurricular activities or clubs that foster positive connections and growth.

Practice Self-Compassion:

Treat yourself with kindness and self-compassion. Avoid harsh self-criticism or negative self-talk. Acknowledge your achievements, no matter how small, and celebrate your progress.

Understand that nobody is perfect, and it's okay to make mistakes or have limitations. Setting realistic expectations for yourself can reduce stress and promote a positive outlook.

Practice Mindfulness and Stress Management:

Incorporate mindfulness practices, such as meditation or deep breathing exercises, into your daily routine. These techniques can help you stay present, reduce stress, and maintain a positive mindset.

Develop effective stress management strategies to cope with academic or personal pressures. This can include time management, goal setting, and seeking support when needed.

Stay Inspired:

Surround yourself with inspirational content, such as books, podcasts, TED Talks, or documentaries that motivate and uplift you in your educational and personal growth journey.

Incorporating these strategies into your life can help you create a positive and nurturing environment for your psychological well-being and education. By surrounding yourself with positivity, you'll be better equipped to overcome challenges, maintain a growth mindset, and achieve your educational and personal development goals.

CHAPTER FOUR

Fixing Your Lack Of Motivation In Business

STEP 1: FINDING THE SOURCE OF SELF-DOUBT

Identifying self-doubt in the context of business and motivation is a critical step in addressing and overcoming it. Self-doubt can undermine your confidence, hinder your decision-making, and impede your progress.

Monitor Your Thoughts and Emotions:

Self-doubt is often accompanied by feelings of anxiety and fear, particularly when you face challenges or opportunities in your business endeavors.

If you find yourself overthinking decisions or constantly seeking validation from others, it may be a sign of self-doubt.

Reflect on Past Experiences:

Think about past instances where self-doubt may have hindered your business or motivational pursuits. Consider whether it prevented you from taking action, pursuing opportunities, or persisting in the face of setbacks.

Conversely, reflect on times when you successfully navigated challenges or achieved your goals. Analyze the role of self-doubt in those situations and how you overcame it.

Assess Your Comfort Zone:

Self-doubt often leads to avoidance behavior. If you consistently avoid tasks or opportunities that could benefit your business or motivation, it may be a sign of underlying self-doubt.

Analyze whether you tend to stay in your comfort zone to avoid facing situations that trigger self-doubt.

Review Decision-Making:

When making business decisions or setting motivational goals, take note of any moments of hesitation or indecision. This could be a sign that self-doubt is influencing your choices.

Frequent second-guessing of your decisions, even after they've been made, is another indicator of self-doubt.

Self-Reflection and Journaling:

Engage in regular self-reflection and journaling to explore your thoughts and emotions. Write down instances when you've experienced self-doubt and try to identify the underlying triggers.

Look for patterns or recurring themes in your self-doubt, such as specific situations, people, or types of challenges that tend to trigger it.

If self-doubt significantly impacts your business and motivation, consider seeking help from a therapist, coach, or counselor. They can provide strategies and support to address the root causes of self-doubt.

Finding the source of self-doubt is the first step towards addressing and overcoming it. Once you recognize the signs and triggers of self-doubt in your business and motivational pursuits, you can work on developing strategies to build self-confidence, challenge negative self-talk, and take proactive steps toward your goals. Overcoming self-doubt is essential for unlocking your full potential and achieving success in your endeavors.

STEP 2: SET VERY CLEAR GOALS

Setting clear goals in the context of business and motivation is essential for guiding your efforts, maintaining focus, and staying motivated to achieve success. Here's a detailed explanation of how to set clear goals effectively:

Define Specific Goals:

Your goals should be specific and well-defined. Instead of a vague goal like "increase sales," specify the exact target, such as "increase monthly sales revenue by 15%."

Ensure that your goals are measurable so that you can track progress and success. For example, if your goal is to expand your customer base, specify the number of new customers you want to acquire.

Set a realistic time-frame for achieving your goals. Having a deadline creates a sense of urgency and helps you stay accountable. For instance, "achieve a 20% increase in website traffic within six months."

Align with Your Business Vision:

Your goals should align with your broader business vision and long-term objectives. They should serve as stepping stones toward the larger picture of what you want your business to become.

Consistency between your goals and vision ensures that you're working toward a cohesive and meaningful purpose, which can be highly motivating.

Make Goals Achievable:

Set goals that are realistic and attainable given your current resources, capabilities, and market conditions. Unrealistic goals can lead to frustration and demotivation.

While goals should be realistic, they should also be challenging enough to inspire effort and growth. Striking the right balance is crucial.

Break Goals into Smaller Steps:

Divide larger goals into smaller, actionable steps or milestones. This makes the path to achieving the larger goal clearer and less overwhelming.

Tracking your progress towards these smaller steps allows you to stay motivated by celebrating achievements along the way.

Identify Key-Performance-Indicators (KPIs):

Determine the key metrics or KPIs that will indicate whether you've successfully achieved your goals. KPIs provide concrete measures of progress and success.

Continuously monitor and analyze these KPIs to ensure you're on track and to make any necessary adjustments to your strategies.

Create an Action Plan:

Develop a detailed action plan that outlines the specific actions, tasks, and resources required to achieve each goal.

Assign responsibilities and deadlines within your team or to yourself to ensure that everyone knows their role in working toward the goals.

Setting clear goals in business and motivation provides direction, focus, and motivation to drive your efforts towards success. When goals are specific, realistic, and aligned with your vision, they become powerful tools for guiding your business endeavors and sustaining your motivation over the long term.

STEP 4: GET AN ACCOUNTABILITY PARTNER

Accountability partners play a crucial role in business and motivation by providing support, encouragement, and a structured framework for achieving goals. Here's a detailed explanation of accountability partners and how they work in the context of business and motivation:

Definition of Accountability Partners:

Accountability partners are individuals who mutually commit to helping each other achieve their respective goals and objectives. This partnership is based on trust, honesty, and shared accountability.

Partners agree to regular check-in meetings or interactions where they discuss progress, challenges, and strategies related to their goals.

Role and Benefits of Accountability Partners:

Accountability partners provide emotional support and encouragement, which can be especially valuable during times of uncertainty or when facing challenging tasks.

Knowing that someone is tracking your progress can boost motivation. You're more likely to stay on track and maintain momentum when you have someone to report to.

Partners help refine and clarify goals by asking questions and providing feedback. This process can lead to more specific and achievable objectives.

When challenges or obstacles arise, accountability partners can offer fresh perspectives and problem-solving ideas. They may have experienced similar issues and can share their insights.

Partners celebrate each others successes, no matter how small. This positive reinforcement can enhance confidence and motivation.

Finding the Right Accountability Partner:

Seek a partner with similar goals or values. While it's not necessary to have identical objectives, shared interests can foster a deeper connection.

Look for someone whose strengths complement your weaknesses. This diversity can offer a more comprehensive perspective on your goals.

Choose someone reliable and committed to the partnership. A partner who consistently shows up and follows through is crucial for accountability.

Effective communication is essential. Make sure you can openly discuss your progress, setbacks, and concerns with your partner.

Setting Up Accountability Structures:

Define your individual and shared goals. Ensure they are specific, measurable, achievable, relevant, and time-bound (SMART).

Decide on a schedule for your accountability meetings. This could be weekly, biweekly, or monthly, depending on your preferences and the nature of your goals.

Determine how you'll track progress. This might involve sharing updates via email, phone calls, video conferences, or using specialized tools or apps.

Effective Accountability Meetings:

During your meetings, review your progress toward your goals. Share both successes and challenges.

Collaborate on finding solutions to any obstacles or setbacks you've encountered. Brainstorm strategies to overcome difficulties.

Adjust your goals if necessary and establish new targets for the upcoming period. Ensure these goals align with your long-term vision.

Acknowledge and celebrate achievements, no matter how small. This positive reinforcement can boost motivation and maintain a positive atmosphere.

Maintaining Accountability:

Stay committed to the partnership. Consistent check-ins and ongoing support are essential for long-term accountability. Be open to adapting your goals and strategies as circumstances change. Flexibility is key to maintaining accountability during unexpected challenges.

Assessing the Accountability Partnership:

Periodically assess the effectiveness of your partnership. Discuss what's working and what needs improvement to ensure the accountability partnership remains beneficial for both parties.

In summary, accountability partners are individuals who collaborate to support each other in achieving their business and motivational goals. They provide emotional support, goal clarity, motivation, problem-solving, and a structured framework for progress. By selecting the right partner, establishing clear goals and accountability structures, and maintaining consistent communication, you can harness the power of accountability to boost your business and motivation.

STEP 5: DON'T BE AFRAID TO CELEBRATE

Celebrating achievements in the context of business and motivation is a crucial practice that can boost morale, increase motivation, and reinforce a positive company culture. Here's a detailed explanation of why and how to celebrate achievements effectively:

Why Celebrate Achievements?

Celebrating achievements recognizes and acknowledges the hard work and dedication of individuals or teams. It validates their efforts and contributions, boosting their self-esteem and job satisfaction.

Celebrations serve as motivators. When employees see their efforts rewarded and recognized, they are more likely to stay engaged, set higher goals, and work harder to achieve them. Celebrating achievements fosters a sense of camaraderie and teamwork. It reinforces the idea that everyone's contributions matter and encourages collaboration within the organization.

Regular celebrations contribute to a positive organizational culture. Employees feel valued and appreciated, leading to greater job satisfaction and lower turnover rates.

How to Celebrate Achievements:

1. Public Recognition:

Share the achievement with the entire team or company through announcements at meetings, newsletters, or on a company bulletin board.

Publicly acknowledge achievements on social media platforms to showcase your team's success and boost company morale.

For personal achievements you should post it if you are looking for recognition in whatever field you are in. Especially if you want to be seen as an authority figure in your niche.

2. Awards and Certificates:

Present awards, certificates, or plaques to individuals or teams who have achieved significant milestones or made outstanding contributions.

In a remote or virtual work setting, create digital certificates or badges to recognize achievements, and share them through email or company platforms.

3. Verbal Appreciation:

Express gratitude and appreciation verbally to the individuals or teams involved. A sincere "thank you" can go a long way in motivating employees.

During meetings or company gatherings, publicly thank and praise those responsible for the achievement.

4. Team Celebrations:

Treat the team to a special lunch or dinner to celebrate their success. It's an excellent opportunity for team bonding and relaxation.

Host themed office parties or gatherings to celebrate achievements. It can be as simple as a cake-cutting ceremony or a more elaborate event.

5. Financial Rewards:

Consider offering performance-based bonuses or incentives as a tangible reward for achieving specific goals or milestones.

If applicable, share a portion of the profits generated from the achievement with the employees who contributed to it.

6. Professional Development:

Offer opportunities for skill development or career advancement as a reward for achievement. This shows a long-term commitment to employee growth.

Consider promoting employees who have consistently demonstrated outstanding performance and contributed significantly to the company's achievements.

7. Flexibility and Recognition:

Provide employees with additional paid time off or flexible work hours as a way to acknowledge their dedication and hard work.

Encourage a healthy work-life balance to show that the company values the well-being of its employees.

8. Customized Recognition:

Consider individual preferences when recognizing achievements. Some employees may prefer public recognition, while others may appreciate a more private acknowledgment.

Offer personalized gifts or tokens of appreciation to show that you've taken the time to consider their interests.

9. Sustainability and Consistency:

Celebrate achievements consistently, not just for major milestones. Recognizing smaller wins keeps motivation high.

Ensure that your celebrations align with your company's values and sustainability efforts. Consider eco-friendly celebrations to reduce environmental impact.

In conclusion, celebrating achievements is a powerful tool for motivation and positive company culture. By recognizing and appreciating the efforts of your team or employees, you not only boost morale but also inspire continued excellence and dedication. Customizing your celebrations and maintaining consistency in recognition efforts can lead to a more motivated and engaged workforce, ultimately benefiting your business's success.

CHAPTER FIVE

Changing Your Ideas On Self-Improvement

STEP 1: SELF-REFLECTION

Self-reflection is a critical practice in the pursuit of self-improvement. It involves taking a deliberate and honest look at yourself, your thoughts, actions, and experiences, to gain insight, learn from past experiences, and make positive changes in your life. Here's a detailed explanation of self-reflection in the context of self-improvement:

Self-Awareness:

Self-reflection starts with understanding who you are, including your values, beliefs, strengths, weaknesses, and motivations. It's about gaining a deep awareness of your own identity and what makes you unique.

Self-reflection helps you develop emotional intelligence by recognizing and understanding your emotions, reactions, and how they influence your behavior and decisions.

The Process of Self-Reflection:

To engage in self-reflection effectively, find a quiet and comfortable space where you can focus without distractions. Writing in a journal is a common and effective way to engage in self-reflection. It allows you to record your thoughts, feelings, and experiences.

Meditation and mindfulness practices can help you become more present in the moment, making it easier to reflect on your thoughts and experiences.

Purpose of Self-Reflection:

Self-reflection helps clarify your goals and aspirations. By examining your values and desires, you can better understand what you want to achieve in life.

When you encounter challenges or setbacks, self-reflection allows you to analyze the situation, identify potential solutions, and make informed decisions.

The primary purpose of self-reflection is to identify areas in your life where you can grow and improve. This might include personal development, skills enhancement, or overcoming negative habits.

Benefits of Self-Reflection:

Self-reflection helps you make more informed and thoughtful decisions. It reduces impulsivity and allows you to consider different perspectives and options.

By understanding your emotions through self-reflection, you can learn to manage them effectively, reducing stress and promoting emotional well-being.
Self-reflection can help you navigate conflicts and improve your relationships by enabling you to see situations from other people's perspectives.

It stimulates creativity and innovation by encouraging you to think critically and explore new ideas and solutions.

The Role of Questions in Self-Reflection:

During self-reflection, ask yourself open-ended questions like "What are my strengths and weaknesses?" or "What could I have done differently in this situation?"

Self-reflection involves questioning your assumptions, beliefs, and biases. It helps you recognize any unhelpful thought patterns and replace them with more positive and constructive ones.

Continuous Process:

Self-reflection is a continuous process that evolves over time. As you learn and grow, your self-reflection practices will adapt to your changing circumstances and goals.

Regular self-reflection enables you to adjust your goals and priorities based on new insights and changing circumstances.

Action-Oriented:

Self-reflection is most effective when it leads to action. After identifying areas for improvement, take concrete steps toward self-improvement and personal growth.

In summary, self-reflection is a powerful tool for self-improvement that involves examining your thoughts, emotions, experiences, and actions to gain insight and make positive changes. It enhances self-awareness, promotes emotional intelligence, and helps you set and achieve meaningful goals. By engaging in regular self-reflection, you can continuously evolve and grow as a person.

STEP 2: AFFIRM THE POSITIVE THINGS

Positive affirmations are powerful self-improvement tools that involve the practice of repeating positive, uplifting statements to oneself with the goal of fostering a more optimistic and constructive mindset.

What Are Positive Affirmations?

Positive affirmations are short, positive, and present-tense statements that are designed to challenge and replace negative or self-limiting thoughts and beliefs. They are typically used to boost self-esteem, enhance confidence, reduce stress and anxiety, and promote a positive outlook on life. Positive affirmations are rooted in the principles of self-talk and self-empowerment.

How to Use Positive Affirmations for Self-Improvement

1. Identify Limiting Beliefs:

Begin by recognizing the negative or self-limiting beliefs that you want to change. These might include thoughts like "I'm not good enough," "I can't do this," or "I always fail."

2. Craft Positive Affirmations:

Create positive affirmations that directly counteract the negative beliefs you've identified. These affirmations should be concise, specific, and framed in the present tense. For example, if you struggle with self-doubt, you might create an affirmation like, "I am confident and capable."

3. Repeat Affirmations Regularly:

Incorporate the practice of repeating your affirmations into your daily routine. You can say them aloud or silently to yourself. Some people find it helpful to write them down in a journal.

Consistency is key. Repeat your affirmations multiple times throughout the day, especially during moments of self-doubt or negative self-talk.

4. Visualization:

As you repeat your affirmations, visualize the positive outcomes associated with them. Imagine yourself living the reality described in your affirmations.

5. Believe in Your Affirmations:

For affirmations to be effective, you must believe in the possibility of the positive outcomes they suggest. It may take time for your subconscious mind to accept and internalize these new beliefs.

6. Be Patient and Persistent:

Self-improvement takes time, and the effects of positive affirmations may not be immediate. Be patient with yourself and continue the practice consistently.

7. Affirmations for Various Areas of Self-Improvement:

Self-Esteem: **"I am worthy of love and respect."**
Confidence: **"I trust myself and my abilities."**
Goal Achievement: **"I am capable of achieving my goals."**
Stress Reduction: **"I am calm, centered, and in control of my emotions."**
Health and Wellness: **"I prioritize my health and make choices that nourish my body."**
Productivity: **"I am focused and productive in my work."**

A powerful self-improvement tool, positive affirmations can help you rewire your mental processes and develop a more optimistic, helpful mindset. They can serve as a catalyst for personal development, boosted self-esteem, and enhanced general well-being when continuously applied and sincerely believed.

STEP 3: GET A PDP

A personal development plan (PDP) is a framework with clear objectives for developing personally. It's an active document that specifies your objectives, points out areas for development, and outlines the activities you'll take to better many facets of your life.

Self-Reflection and Assessment:

Decide what you want to accomplish in each area of your life to start. Career, education, health, relationships, personal growth, and other topics may fall under this category.

Consider your advantages and disadvantages. Think about the abilities and traits you have that can help you reach your goals and the areas where you need to improve.

Define your priorities and values. Recognize what is most important to you because this will help you develop goals.

Identify Action Steps:

Organize your objectives into manageable, smaller steps. These acts or duties ought to be precise ones that advance you toward your objectives.

Choose which sequence you'll do these tasks in. Prioritize chores that are important first.

Seek Resources and Support:

Determine the abilities, information, or resources you require to accomplish your objectives. This can entail looking for mentorship, training, or further education. Think about the people who can assist and direct. This may be friends, relatives, mentors, or coaches who can keep you accountable and inspired.

Create a Timeline:

Create a schedule outlining the dates you intend to finish each step of your personal development plan. You can stay organized and on schedule by doing this.

Review and Adjust as Needed:

Review and revise your personal development plan frequently. Your strategy can need modifications as you reach your goals and as your circumstances alter.

A personal development plan is, in essence, a methodical strategy to self-improvement and personal development. You can lay out a plan for ongoing self-improvement by defining SMART goals, breaking them down into manageable steps, looking for resources and assistance, keeping track of your progress, and remaining motivated.

A well-designed PDP can give you the tools you need to realize your goals and live a more fulfilled life.

STEP 5: BE SUPER PERSISTENT

Being persistent in seeking for self-improvement is essential for long-term success and personal development. It entails persistently pursuing self-development despite barriers, setbacks, or difficulties.

Commitment and Motivation

Discover your inner motivation and drive. Recognize the importance of self-improvement in your own life. Even when external elements are less helpful, this internal drive will keep you persistent.

Keep your vision and goals clear. To remind yourself of your goals, write them down, make vision boards, or utilize daily affirmations.

Embrace Consistency

Focus on creating regular routines that support your personal development objectives. The secret to long-lasting improvement in these behaviors is consistency.
Include self-improvement pursuits in your weekly or daily schedule. This makes them seem more normal in your life.

Learn from Setbacks

Recognize that the road to improvement includes setbacks and failures. Build resiliency and see these difficulties as learning opportunities.

Analyze what went wrong after failures, take lessons from them, and modify your strategy as necessary.

Adapt and Evolve

Be willing to change your objectives and tactics as you gain knowledge and experience. Your path for self-improvement could change over time.

Adopt a growth mindset and continue to learn. Look for new knowledge and abilities that will benefit your self-improvement efforts.

Self-Compassion

Develop self-forgiveness and self-compassion. Be gentle with yourself if you experience a few setbacks or make a slow start.

To increase your confidence and keep a positive outlook, use affirmations and positive self-talk.

Long-Term Perspective

Recognize that self-improvement requires sustained effort. Understand that lasting transformation requires time and that there are no fast cures.

Accept the idea that you can always improve yourself. Continue establishing new goals even after you reach your first set in order to continue developing and progressing. It takes commitment, perseverance, and a strong belief in one's own ability to develop oneself.

You may overcome hurdles and obstacles on your path to becoming your greatest self by making clear goals, staying consistent, learning from setbacks, getting assistance, and practicing self-compassion. Keep in mind that tenacity is the secret to real and permanent transformation.

CONCLUSION

In the course of "Breaking the Stone Wall: Get Rid of the Beliefs That Ruin Your Life and Your Business," we've investigated the profound influence that our beliefs can have on our lives, touching on a variety of topics like physical activity, fitness injury prevention, psychology education, training, business motivation, and self-improvement. We have taken the risk of removing the hurdles that earlier posed as significant roadblocks in our way with great optimism and resolve.

We have discovered throughout the pages of this book that our behaviors are shaped by our ideas, which may either be powerful or limiting. We have learned how crucial it is to be self-aware in order to identify these ideas and the ways to disprove and change them into allies.

We have learned the value of persistent effort and the necessity of setting reasonable goals in the context of exercise and fitness. We have built the foundation for a better, more active life by making the effort to recognize and challenge our limiting beliefs.

We now know that knowledge and good technique are our best partners in the fight against fitness injury. We have protected ourselves against harm via knowledge and awareness of our bodies, ensuring that our physical pursuits continue to be both satisfying and sustainable.

In this field of psychology education, we have embraced the idea of a growth mindset, acknowledging that there is no end to our ability for learning and self-improvement. We have learned that we can conquer any challenge in our way if we have the correct attitude and are dedicated to lifelong learning.

We have seen firsthand how having defined objectives and constant commitment can improve a training environment. In order to drive ourselves toward achievement, we have harnessed the power of accountability and positive reinforcement.

We have tapped into the source of our inner drive in the area of business motivation, encouraging a tireless pursuit of our objectives. We have discovered that motivation is a nurtured mental state that is essential for success in our professional pursuits rather than a passing sensation.

We are on a never-ending quest for progress and self-discovery in the area of self-improvement. With the understanding that each event advances our personal development, we have cherished our victories and drawn lessons from our failures.

As we draw to a close, keep in mind that the road to tearing down the wall of limiting ideas is still open. It is a route that demands perseverance, compassion for oneself, and a firm belief in your ability to alter both your life and your business. Any belief that dares to stand in your way may be disproved because you have the means, the know-how, and the fortitude to do it.

May the knowledge contained within these pages act as a lighthouse for you as you travel toward a life free from the restrictions of artificial limitations. With each myth you disprove, you make room for limitless development, limitless potential, and an unbounded future. You have the ability to mold your life and your company anyway you want. Break free, and may your adventure lead to unbounded fulfillment and expansion.